STRUGGLING TIMES

OTHER BOOKS BY LOUIS SIMPSON

Poetry

The Arrivistes: Poems 1940–1949
Good News of Death and Other Poems
A Dream of Governors
At the End of the Open Road
Selected Poems
Adventures of the Letter I
Searching for the Ox
Armidale
Caviar at the Funeral
The Best Hour of the Night
People Live Here: Selected Poems 1940–1983
Collected Poems
In the Room We Share
Jamaica Poems
There You Are
Nombres et poussière
Kaviar på begravningen
The Owner of the House: New Collected Poems 1940–2001

Literary Criticism

James Hogg: A Critical Study
Three on the Tower: The Lives and Works of Ezra Pound, T.S. Eliot
     and William Carlos Williams
A Revolution in Taste: Studies of Dylan Thomas, Allen Ginsberg, Sylvia
     Plath and Robert Lowell
A Company of Poets
The Character of the Poet
Ships Going into the Blue

Other

Riverside Drive, a novel
North of Jamaica, autobiography
An Introduction to Poetry
Selected Prose, autobiography, fiction, literary criticism
The King My Father's Wreck, autobiography
Moderns Poets of France: A Bilingual Anthology
François Villon: The Legacy & The Testament, translation

STRUGGLING TIMES

poems by

LOUIS SIMPSON

AMERICAN POETS CONTINUUM SERIES, NO. 115

BOA Editions, Ltd. ▣ Rochester, NY ▣ 2009

First Edition
09 10 11 12   7 6 5 4 3 2 1

For information about permission to reuse any material from this book please contact
The Permissions Company at www.permissionscompany.com or e-mail permdude@
eclipse.net.

Publications by BOA Editions, Ltd.—a not-for-profit corporation under section 501 (c) (3)
of the United States Internal Revenue Code—are made possible with funds from a variety of
sources, including public funds from the New York State Council on the Arts, a state agency;
the Literature Program of the National Endowment for the Arts; the County of Monroe, NY;
the Lannan Foundation for support of the Lannan Translations Selection Series; the Sonia
Raiziss Giop Charitable Foundation; the Mary S. Mulligan Charitable Trust; the Roches-
ter Area Community Foundation; the Arts & Cultural Council for Greater Rochester; the
Steeple-Jack Fund; the Ames-Amzalak Memorial Trust in memory of Henry Ames, Semon
Amzalak and Dan Amzalak; and contributions from many individuals nationwide.

See Colophon on page 88 for special individual acknowledgments.

Cover Design: Sandy Knight
Cover Painting: "La Croix on Red" by Steve Carpenter
Interior Design and Composition: Richard Foerster
Manufacturing: BookMobile
BOA Logo: Mirko

Library of Congress Cataloging-in-Publication Data

Simpson, Louis Aston Marantz, 1923–
Struggling times : poems / by Louis Simpson. — 1st ed.
    p. cm. — (American poets continuum series ; no. 115)
ISBN 978-1-934414-19-4 (trade paper)
I. Title.

PS3537.I75S77 2009
811'.54—dc22

2008042874

NATIONAL
ENDOWMENT
FOR THE ARTS
A great nation
deserves great art.

BOA Editions, Ltd.
Nora A. Jones, Executive Director/Publisher
Thom Ward, Editor/Production
Peter Conners, Editor/Marketing
Glenn William, BOA Board Chair
A. Poulin, Jr., Founder (1938–1996)
250 North Goodman Street, Suite 306
Rochester, NY 14607
www.boaeditions.org

Contents

STRUGGLING TIMES

Struggling Times

One hour they lay buried beneath the ruins of that hall;
But as the stars rise from the salt lake they arise in pain,
In troubled mists o'erclouded by the terrors of struggling times.

—William Blake, *Europe, A Prophecy*

1

We have lost our investments.
The pillars of the kingdom are broken.
This morning's *New York Times*

reports that the ongoing
criminal investigation
is expanding to the banks

that have flown to Bermuda.
Once you could get a basket
of worms and go fishing,

but the rivers too are polluted.
So we shall stay at home
and on Sunday go to church

and hear the priest, who is young
and recently married, preach
on sin and love, and the difference.

2

At the meeting of the Senate
Judiciary Committee
Mr. Kilov, a biologist,

said that the treaties were only paper,
and inspections were useless.
A weapon of mass destruction

could be made by a few professionals,
biologists and chemists, working
in a small, hidden space.

3

You have to be careful
what you hear or see.
In Afghanistan I saw

the man and the woman
who were caught in adultery
buried up to their heads.

Their children were brought
and told to throw stones.
I can still see the heads

twisting on the ground.
The poor devil in *Papillon*
with his head in the guillotine . . .

but Goya's half-buried dog
looking up at the sky
I think was the worst of all.

Suddenly

The truck came at me,
I swerved
but I got a dent.

The car insurance woman
informs me that my policy
has been cancelled.

I say, "You can't do that."
She gives me a little smile
and goes back to her nails.

Lately have you noticed
how aggressively people drive?
A *whoosh!* and whatever.

Some people are suddenly
very rich, and as many
suddenly very poor.

As for the war, don't get me started.
We were too busy watching
the ball game to see

that the things we care about
are suddenly disappearing,
and that they always were.

Avalon

"There's a place named Avalon
where you could walk."

She shows me the map.
"I'll find it," I say.

"I'll just drive around.
I'll find it. I don't need a map."

I have driven around
half the roads on Long Island.

Finally I come to a dead stop
at the sea.

I'm such a fool.
I should have taken the map.

What will I say to her
when I get back?

As it happens, I don't have to.
She says it was . . . clever,

doing what I did. Nothing
is more beautiful than the sea.

A New Year's Child

He wants me to carry him.
It's an order, and I obey.

Though it isn't easy . . .
he twists and turns in my arms,

he wants to see everything
in the world all at once.

Where are his parents?
The man and the woman

talking so seriously . . .
The man leans over and gives her

a kiss on the cheek.
The child looks at me

as if to say, "Did you see that?"
and he laughs.

I could carry this child
forever, he feels so light.

A Spot on the Kitchen Floor

A spot was moving slowly
across the kitchen floor.

I placed a card in front of it.
The bug, for such it was,

climbed on, and continued
to move . . . without legs

apparently, like a toy.
I tilted the card,

and the bug went wild,
running in a circle,

and back to the door,
where it vanished.

There's nothing much doing
here. We might have talked.

An Impasse

Jacques writes from Paris,
"What are the latest news?"

I have told him, time
and time again, "What are"

is not English, "news"
is not plural, "news"

is a singular term, as in "The news is good."

He replies, "Though 'The news'
may be singular in America,

it is not so in France.
Les nouvelles is a plural term.

To say, 'The news is good'
in France would be bad grammar,

and absurd, which is worse.
On the other hand, 'What are

the news?' makes perfect sense."

Tall Girl Running

*There is no gene which single-handedly builds a leg, long or
short. Building a leg is a multi-gene cooperative enterprise.*

—Richard Dawkins

She went running by.
I never saw a girl

with such long legs.
She ran by again.

I shouted to her,
"You run like an angel."

She smiled and said,
"Thank you."

She did some knee bends.
I said, "Where did you

get those legs?"
"My father," she said,

and went her way smiling.

The Liar

She left a car top down
in the rain, and lied about it,

so I knew she was a liar.
And there was nobody

I really wanted to kiss,
so I kissed her.

The caddy is saying,
"Miss Baker moved the ball,"

though later he retracted.
I can still see her . . .

"So sue me! I'm a liar!"

A Time of War

1

JOSHUA CHAMBERLAIN

Some of the men were saying
their enlistment time was up.
They weren't going any farther.

Chamberlain said, in that case,
they wouldn't have to fight,
but they would have to follow,

and they couldn't take their weapons.
After a while at Gettysburg
they asked for their weapons back.

*

He was wounded six times,
awarded the Medal of Honor.
But he spoke of the battles

of the Confederate army,
naming them one by one
as though they were his own.

Where do such old men go
when their lives are over?
I would dearly like to know.

2

BATTLEFIELDS

At Fredricksburg
the Union army
attacks Marye's Hill.
Thousands are dead or dying.

Hundreds are killed
every minute at Cold Harbor.
They write on a piece of paper,
"Bury me here."

What drives them to kill
or be killed?
To get it over with.
Fear is not as strong as this.

3

OLD MEN TALKING

A general named Grant
waited with his army
by the roadside to receive
the surrender of General Lee.

Lee arrived finally,
bedecked and bemedaled
in his only good uniform.
He and Grant shook hands.
Finally they got round to eat.

The Confederates hadn't eaten
in weeks. They would be fed.
Officers could keep their side arms.

A man was going to blow a bugle
to celebrate the surrender,
but Grant put a stop to it.
It wasn't a surrender,
just two old men talking.

The Confederate army
stood at attention.
The line of ragged men
would have been quite willing
to have their war all over again.

Ishi

Ishi, the last of his tribe,
walked out of the forest.
He was dying of starvation.
A home was found for him,
the Anthropology Museum,
and harmless occupations.

He helped the hospital nurses
clean their instruments.
He showed Professor Kroeber
his tools: a pot for cooking,
a rope, a basket,
a bow and arrow.

*

Ishi liked to walk to town
and ride the trolley.
Kroeber took him to the opera.
Instead of watching the show
Ishi turned his chair around
and looked at the crowd.

The first airplane he saw
made exploding noises.
"American man go up
in sky," he said, and laughed,
like an ancient Roman,
not to be astonished by anything.

*

Ishi died of tuberculosis.
He was buried with five arrows,

"some things of a personal nature,"
and left the noisy world
as quietly as he came,
taking the forest with him.

My Life the Movie

His is nattily dressed
like a French officer,
in a uniform with boots.

A woman with long black hair
comes in. She looks distracted.
She runs toward him,

and clasps him in her arms.
He stands stock still,
and the director shouts, "Cut!"

*

A conference is in progress.
An older man with gray hair,
the CEO, is in charge.

"You took your time getting here,"
says one of the conferees,
and laughs. He's no friend of mine.

But the CEO smiles,
and the faces turned to me
at the long table are smiling.

*

I have ideas
that seem so real
that the characters,

who I have never seen,
must be alive somewhere.
If I went there, they would be:

the unmoving Frenchman,
the beautiful, distracted girl,
the smiling, gray-haired CEO.

Sentimental Education

He first fell in love
when he was sixteen.

To hear him tell it, she
was the Aphrodite surfing

ashore on a seashell.
He never got over her.

Though, Lord knows, he tried,
with others who weren't

"his type." Never again!
Ah, the alimony, the pain!

*

Someone has given his heart
a jump start.

It is running again.
What a wonderful feeling!

He won't make the same
stupid mistakes twice.

This time will be different.
Anyhow, it's not as if he

were falling in love.
What has he to lose?

*

He used to be smart,
liked to listen to Buxtehude,

or at least Mozart.
Now he showers to Cole Porter.

What does he see in her?
What does she see in him?

"The peasant who pleases one
is better off than the king

with a thousand beautiful wives
who doesn't," said Solomon.

The Man on the Pulley

I wait in the chapel
for fifteen minutes.

Then go with my walker
to Rehabilitation,
and do a few exercises.
They hurt like hell.

I watch Mike working
with the man on the pulley.
He was in a car crash
and smashed his legs in pieces.
In fact he would have died,
but the doctor worked on him
and put the bones together.
"He is the toughest man,"
Mike says, "I have ever known."

I watch Mike sliding magazines
under one of the legs, to make it
even with the other.
The man is a likable fellow.
I am filled with envy.
I would like to be as tough
as he is, but I'm not . . .
as if something is gnawing
on my leg, and it doesn't end.

It seems that finally
life is real, not a joke.

What would it be like
to be nailed to a cross?

I won't hear the bones splinter.

On Lake Champlain

1

My cousin Jenny lived
in Burlington, Vermont.
She and her husband Charles
rented a house on the lake.

The back yard was large.
You had to sit on the lawn mower to drive it.

The road to the house was curved,
dusty and full of rocks.
The car bounced its way to the house.
There were many trees. It looked dismal.

But a light was shining through a window,
and a vase standing in a corner.

2

Winter was desolate.
People would stay in their homes for months
without seeing anyone else.
They drank too much.
Some even killed themselves.
Jenny told stories
about people being frozen to death.

3

Then you could see new life beginning,
families of ducks and swans,
flowers blooming,
college students on the lake,

some falling into the lake.
Some people claimed that they saw
the Loch Ness monster.

The shopkeepers polished their floors,
Pakistanis and Indians banking and laughing,
buying up all the houses.

The other side of the lake was Canada.
You didn't have to go through immigration,
you just hopped on the ferry.

The college students hung out sheets
from dormitory windows,
girls waved bras and underwear.
Tourists drove through town,
lawns and houses were manicured.

4

Charles ran a sandwich shop,
egg salad was a specialty.

College students frequented the store
at all hours of the day.
Life was good.

But the man who owned the store died.
The house was sold,
Charles and Jenny moved to Arizona.

Jenny isn't happy,
she's afraid of scorpions.
They are everywhere, she's told.

She misses the egg salad.

Consolations

Dickinson had a cockatoo
she called Semiramis
and loved dearly.

Whitman was a trencherman,
his favorite dish
a mulligan stew.

Frost went for long walks.
Eliot played croquet.
Pound took fencing lessons.

There is a snapshot of Yeats
with a woman in a garden,
naked to the waist and smiling.

Auden, when he was old,
counted the sheets of toilet paper
that a visitor used.

Nevertheless

A man lived by himself,
but he needed someone

to mend his clothes.
There was a woman

he heard of who sewed.
He brought her his clothes,

an old Spanish woman
with a funny nose.

But she did a good job.
So he asked her again,

and again, but
the next time he asked,

she said, "It depends."
She mended the clothes

nevertheless.
So what would it depend on?

The next time he went
it happened again.

He brought clothes to her,
she said, "It depends,"

but she mended the clothes.
He couldn't resist.

"What did it depend on?"
he asked. The old woman

stood up, turned around,
"On this" . . . put her arms

around him, gave him
a kiss, and

he fled.

*

He told a friend about it.
"Did you ever go back?"

"Do you think I'm crazy?"
"Not even for your clothes?"

So he went back.
There the old woman sat.

She said, "I was wondering
when you would come

to pick up your clothes."
She seemed to be

not in the least embarrassed.
And so life went on

as it usually does.

With Best Wishes

Every Christmas I get a card
from Dave. It has a picture
of him and Maureen, four sons,

and all the wives and children.
Dave and I were buddies
in the East Village long ago.

He was doing a series of paintings:
the Chrysler Building
at different times of day.

He threw the brush down, "Screw Monet!"
and went over
and pissed in the kitchen sink.

*

The Christmas card has come.
The children look the blooming
picture of perfect health.

Maureen is wearing the pearls
Dave gave her on a birthday,
and Dave wears a wide smile.

In Old New Orleans

A man and woman
go by, pushing a pram.
The *Times* has arrived.

I go down in pajamas.
The city is under water,
suddenly drowned.

It used to be dripping
as leisurely as a cave
or an old cathedral.

Where are we going?
Some smart machine
rips off an answer.

"Greed will grow
and hatred make
the world a hell."

But the damned ego
comes whining back,
and it all starts again.

Chamber Music

1

Anne-Louise Boivin d'Hardancourt
was unhappy.
Her husband, Jacques Brillon,
had a mistress. Of all people,
the children's governess!

She shed some tears.
But Brillon's absurd behavior
gave her leave to please herself.

She wanted to meet Doctor Franklin,
the most famous man in Paris.
He was said to like Scotch airs,
and wrote a regimental march
celebrating the Battle of Saratoga.

2

She composed chamber music
and played the harpsichord.
She expressed a wish to have
some sheets of the music
that Doctor Franklin liked.

Anne-Louise d'Hardancourt.
was one of the most beautiful
women in Paris . . .
golden hair, "doe eyes," a figure
of the kind Doctor Franklin liked.

She was a cultured woman.
She had read Plato,

The Encyclopédie, Racine.
Getting her to bed
would be no simple matter.

3

But he found a way.
He spoke of making love
as though it were only
an amusement . . . her virtue
as though it were unassailable.

She invited him to visit
her estate in the country.
After his second visit
she called him "Papa"
and would sit in his lap.

People criticized her for it.
She wouldn't apologize for anything.
She called it her "sweet habit."

Ah, Paris! Ah, Liberty!
What fun there used to
be before the Revolution,
Monsieur Guillotine,
and *grand guignol.*

4

So Anne-Louise
is sitting on his knee,
or his lap. This isn't clear.

He has been with many women.
That wasn't a sin . . .

but he must never again
make love to anyone else.
Now that we have that settled,

there are other things to be done.
Ben has been appointed to
the royal commission.
He must not think she loves him less
because she sits in his lap less often.

5

He was old. And it was time
he returned to his own country.
It was a triumphant march,
the coach sank on the springs
so many came to say good-bye.

But not Anne-Louise.
It would have been like tearing
the heart out of her body.

He disliked writing letters,
but he wrote to her.
Her absence, he said,
instead of diminishing,
only augmented his desire.

The Catalogue

I did not order it,
yet it arrives,
a catalogue of books,
each subject described
in red letters, above
the title in black.

The name of the author
below in smaller type . . .
as authors should be,
reserving large capital letters
for writers of cookbooks and bestsellers.
A rapid perusal
leaves me . . . impressed.
I can have *Liberty, Order, and Justice*
for twenty dollars or twelve . . .
hardcover or paperback.

Here is an author I knew:
Pufendorf, "founding father
of the doctrine of toleration."
I once put Pufendorf in a poem,
thinking the name was funny.
The catalogue tells me he was
a *von* Pufendorf, no less.

Lectures on the French Revolution
by John Emerich Edward Dalberg-Acton . . .
I used to refer to him
familiarly as Acton.
I never shall again.

The Collected Works of
James M. Buchanan
in twenty volumes . . .

I could go on and on,
but am saddened not just
by the memory of my impertinence

but the thought of all the great books
I have not read, and the subjects
I know nothing about, really,
and now it is much too late.

Lord, how they could write!
It would have been helpful
to have read Helmut Schoeck
on envy at least.

Mr. and Mrs. Yeats

"The common condition
of our life," Yeats said,
"is hatred."

You might think as he did
if you loved a woman
who never would love you,
an angry, shouting woman,
a woman like Maud Gonne.

And if instead of love
you had "theater business,"
and your better moments
were at the club, "exchanging
polite meaningless words."

But then, suppose you met
a women, oddly named,
who had a kinder face.
George helped him understand
the phases of the moon.

She talked to the great dead
in automatic writing.
Yeats and his wife together
went up a winding stair
that leads. . . I don't know where.

(It wasn't a religion,
Yeats despised religion.)
The point is, he discovered
the common life of man
and woman could be kind.

And if it wasn't love,
as love is in the movies,
they didn't seem to mind.

Joan Crawford Was Right

Joan Crawford was right
about the wire coat hangers,
not to have them in the house.

They come with the shirts,
go to the closet, and quietly
hang on a bar. Then the shirts
go back to the dry cleaners, one
by one, until the last shirt is gone.

Now the wire coat hangers
have the room to themselves.
Then it begins . . . on the bar,
the shuffling of empty hangers.
They are moving from the closet

to the floor. It is astonishing
how the pile of hangers grows,
in twos, tangled with each other.
You think about them a great deal.
But you can't procrastinate forever. . . .

You sit yourself down one day
and put wire hangers in bunches,
the hooks all facing the same way.
You never want to see another wire
hanger. You have a life of your own.

So you tie them with twist ties,
and drive them in a Hefty bag
back to the cleaners. The woman
doesn't thank you, as if every day
she is given hangers tied like these.

In a Declivity

Where is the one who makes me laugh?
Why did she go up a hill

and through the door of a closet?
They were working in a declivity,

burly pick and shovel men.
The centipede I saw was poisonous.

Why was I standing in a declivity?
I had been shot down.

A boy ran into the house
and came out again,

extending a cigarette case.
I said, "Thanks, old man."

I must give up my old movies.
Nobody likes what I dream.

The Constant Reader

I do not see the plays
and miss all the operas.

Let those who must love.
As Chaucer says, "What sholde

I bye it on my flesh so deere?"
The truth is, I prefer

to read.

Doctor Goodman

1
DOCTOR GOODMAN'S THEATER

"It is cold," Stanley says.
"Shut up," says Johnson.

Latah is making faces.
He says, "Who am I now?"

"The wind is cold," Stanley says.
"Fool," says Johnson.

"I am very cold," Stanley says.
"Damn fool," says Johnson.

*

"You made nurse Thompson cry.
Don't say you didn't mean to,"

says smiling Doctor Goodman.
"You've been a bad boy, Latah."

Stanley, Johnson, Latah,
and Doctor himself are happy

to be taking part in the play,
each man mad in his own way.

2
DOCTOR GOODMAN'S DISPASSION

He has just been reading
about "paradoxical

hyperthermia."
The traveler is caught

in a snow storm. He's freezing.
The last whisper of heat

in the body kicks in.
It's a good feeling.

He feels nice and warm.
He is starting to sweat

and lies down in the snow.
"Goodman, what's the paradox?"

"How relieved he must be,
almost happy in the end."

3
THE DEVIL AND DOCTOR GOODMAN

"Good evening, Doctor Goodman,
this may amuse you.

I have just been talking
to a man who believes in god.

In these enlightened times!
A god who drowns the world

and fishes it up again!"
"I know," said Doctor Goodman.

"You frighten little children
and Hell-tormented men

and women, not a few.
Where does it ever get you?

Life is always moving,
and love is ever new."

The Glass Eel Gatherer

We were watching the team
at practice—counting to ten,
running at each other,
colliding in helmets,
and falling down again.

Was she a fan?

Hardly, she said.
She was taking a break
from her job, biology,
i.e., glass eels.

They were transparent.
She was doing research,
counting and measuring. Actually
Europeans consider them
a delicacy.

"Europeans!" I snorted,
and she laughed.

I was considering her.
But she had a friend . . .
she mentioned him twice.
So that was that. She returned
to the country of Might Have Been.

But whenever I'm feeling
out of sorts for some reason . . .
a serial murderer
has been given a parole

for good behavior.
Or the generals are sure
they have everything in hand.

Or the fact that nobody
in the world gives a damn
for anything I think or do . . .
Will there still be Medicare

when I am old? Will I be able
to lean over and tie my shoes?

I see myself in one room
with all my books, and no one
to talk to but Proust, and he's dead.

At such times I think about her,
my lovely glass eel gatherer.
She is down by the water,
in her waders and her shorts,
and a shirt that is wet
and transparent.

She is standing perfectly still,
looking down at the water.
Then she stoops and carefully
stands up with something,
a vessel, in her hands,
and brings it, and shows me
glass eels.

Wheels

The Egyptians changed their minds
about letting the Jews go.

The Egyptians came riding
with their chariots and spears,

and horses. Let's not forget
the poor bloody horses.

A big wave came rolling,
the Egyptians drowned,

and Moses led the people
to freedom. That's how it goes.

The wheels! Look at the wheels,
chariots rusting in the sun.

Who imagined the wheels?
There must have been someone

right from the beginning,
the world without end.

Good Hope, Where Are You?

Father took me to the movies.
A warship was sinking,

and the Captain calling,
"Good Hope, where are you?"

I had an ocean liner,
a hammer and a nail.

I made a warship sinking.
At night when he came home

and saw what I had done
I thought he would be angry,

but he just smiled and said,
"What a war it must have been!"

Astronomers in Arizona

"Astronomers in Arizona
are racing to build the biggest
telescope ever."

Why are they racing?
What do they hope to find?
There are no other worlds . . .

This is it, Old Moon Face.
It may be fun to fly around,
but don't expect to meet anyone

you haven't met already.
The telescope, says the *Times*,
will have "concave mirrors."

Bully for you! Astronomers
live in a world of their own.
What have we to do with it?

When the "learn'd astronomer,"
made him sick, Whitman says,
"I wander'd off by myself . . .

and from time to time,
look'd up in perfect
silence at the stars."

The Excursion

Many were walking
in the same direction.
Some were young,
others middle-aged,
and some were old.

It was growing dark
and they were cold.
They were going back
when somebody said
that they were lost.

That they all were going
in the wrong direction . . .
Fortunately

someone had a compass.
There was a sigh of relief.
It would have been
a fearful thing
to be lost in the dark.

There was nothing to fear.
It was a cloudless night
and the moon was shining.
Everyone was glad,
and a voice spoke and said,

"Ye are gods,
and all of you children
of the most High."

Beatrice

She could not read music
but taught herself to sing.

Today, all over the world
people listen to her songs.

Her mother says, "I think
Beatrice needs a husband."

Her father says, "Why? I
don't see why she should."

The parrot hangs around.
Sooner or later someone

will give Polly a cracker.
Beatrice talks to her and

sings. It's a good life. If
we think so, anything is.

The Burned Man

This is the burned man.
He walks with his arm in a sling.

He doesn't remember anything.
There ought to be a shield

or cover of some kind.
He looks in every direction,

but there is nothing.

He thinks he hears voices
and talking, far away.

If there is a bright spot on the skin,
and the bright spot stays in place,

and does not spread,
but remains somewhat dark,

it is the ascension of the burn,
and the priest shall pronounce him clean.

In and About the House

THE OLD-CLOTHES MAN

The man to pick up old clothes
appears to have forgotten.

The bags are waiting for him.
When a car goes by, or a truck,

they wave and flap.
I have been expecting him

for hours. I telephoned.
The woman who lives there said

he has been known not to come
until the very last minute.

The old-clothes man did not come.
I took the bags back to the house

and put them where I would not
hear them crying.

BURNING

I turn on the oven,
but the newspaper comes,

and I start reading.
The next thing I know

is a smell of burning . . .
the saucepan welded

to oatmeal. The bottom
as black as hell.

Should I throw it away?
To hell with that!

It takes me four days scraping,
Dawn, a knife, and steel wool,

but the inside is shining.
There is a network of fine lines.

It feels that it has been scraped,
a bit rough but good as new,

and in fact I like it better.

Vivien in The Waste Land

"Do
"You know nothing? Do you see nothing? Do you remember
"Nothing?"

—T.S. Eliot, *The Waste Land*

That nothing was mine, along with the closed car at four,
and the Cockney woman in the pub. One or two other places, I don't
recall. I wasn't exactly keeping a count, you know.

The bit about nothing? Oh that was something, I said to Tom,
trying to stir him up. It was another rainy night in good old London
Town, and he was sitting still and saying nothing. He'd come home
from the bank worn out. Half an hour for dinner, a nap, and he'd be at
another of his pieces about Webster or Middleton, Lord knows what.
I don't know how he'd find something to say about them. I loved the
poems but I couldn't stand his essays. Literary criticism . . .

I was still a young woman and men found me attractive. Bertie
did. I wanted to get a rise out of Tom. It was though I wasn't there,
just some damned Elizabethan . . . Middleton, Webster, Beaumont
and Fletcher . . . Lord, I hated them with their codpieces and hats with
a feather in it. I said that if he had an idea would he let me in on it.
He just stared. . . miles away in cloud-cuckoo-land. So I said, "Don't
you know anything?" trying to stir him up. They had said I should
try to stimulate him. He changed the way I said it, of course. . . he
made it, "Do you know nothing?" which is very different, isn't it?

I was needling him, but he put it in the poem. I must say it's
better the way he has it . . . it's more significant. It's the Dark Night
of the Soul and all that side of things. He made nothing a thing you
can see. It's empty and dark. He turned it into poetry.

Did I walk in the rain with my hair down so? What do you
take me for, a fool? That was an idea I had to scare him. More than
anything he hated to be embarrassed. He put that about my hair in
the poem too. He knew what to put in and what to leave out.

The Discovery of Silence

The Canon at Law
went into the chapel
and saw Sister Ursula.

She seemed to be praying,
then he saw she was not,
but standing in silence

in front of the book
and moving her lips.
So Sister was ordered

to appear and explain.
She said, "I was saying
the words to myself."

There followed the cure
of scourging and diet
by herself in a cell.

It happened again.
This time she was burned
to save her from hell.

*

Unable to rest
we wander amazed
by candles and shadows.

Pray for forgiveness.
Listen to the word
that is heard in silence.

The Caprichos

With a needle
on a metal plate
Goya etches a man
who has been garroted
by the Spanish Inquisition.
The left leg is relaxed,
the right as stiff as a board,
the big toe sticking out at an angle.

"It's better than being hanged,"
Goya says. I shall try to believe it.

Ah, the witches,
the old ones, and the young,
voluptuously naked,
learning to ride a broom.

Would you like to see
an enormous laughing woman
with dropsy? Or the cannibals?
One has cut off a man's hand,
and his head,
and is dancing with them.

Goya paints what he sees.
He doesn't believe in God.

*

Bandits have captured a wagon
and are killing the occupants.
One is on his knees, begging them
to spare his life. Fat chance!

A woman who was raped is now
being stabbed. Her mouth is
wide open, emitting
horrible sounds.

Another of the women
is surpassingly beautiful.
She is being stripped naked.
She turns her face aside,
ashamed of her body,
of what it will do to her.

Goya paints the truth,
what simply and directly is.

*

The father of Saint Anthony of Padua
was said to have murdered a man
in Lisbon. The Saint was transported
directly to Lisbon.

There were two witnesses,
men who had seen the murder.
They had since died,
but Anthony raised these dead
and took them to court
and had them state before judges
whether his father was guilty.
They said he was not.
Anthony's father was set free,
and the dead returned to their graves.

Goya painted the angels
flying about in the Church
of Saint Anthony of Padua.

Are angels male or female?
Hard to say. They are attractive.
There is a flutter of angels,
looking down in the dome,
pointing out things to one another.
A shawl of a striking color . . .
"Let me see, I hadn't noticed,"
one says. She looks sixteen.

This angel was painted by Goya
who doesn't believe in God.

The Omen

Pushkin had a beautiful wife.
A man named d'Anthès
was flirting with Natalya.

Pushkin challenged him to a duel.
On the day appointed
he turned back to do something.

As everyone knows,
once you've set out
to go back is a fateful omen.

*

All Petersburg was out
to enjoy the fine weather.
A friend saw him and waved.

So the men had their duel,
and Pushkin was shot.
He died three days later.

"He didn't hold with omens,"
the gatekeeper said
with a smile and shake of the head.

Jabez

Cloaked reports of shotguns . . .
all the fathers are out,

birds flying over.
I'm tugging at the trigger

of the little shotgun
Rosalind never used,

but it doesn't move.
Baldpate and Whitewing

are flying past.
"Yuh got de savety on,"

Jabez says, and shows me.
I'm too tired to walk,

so Jabez carries me
all the way back.

I don't say thank you
to Jabez. He's my friend.

Eureka Road

The Sherwood Foresters
marched up King Street.

We stood and watched.
I had an old stick

that looked like a gun.
Someone threw it away.

I watched the garden boy
cooking salt fish and ackee

over four stones.
He was telling stories

about Brer Anansi,
Brer Tiger, Brer Alligator.

But Aunt May was calling
"Cooee! Cooee!"

the Australian bush call.
Jonathan said, "Yuh Aunty

gwine tink mi mek yuh black.
Yuh betta guh back."

1234567

All God's children
go to heaven.

Good pinochle players?
And why not?

People on the train with
loud voices and a cellphone—

fakes, showing off?
In His good time

all sins will be forgiven.
Tax collectors.

Will they go to heaven too?
All, all will be forgiven,

with one exception—
a man named Derrida

who taught deconstruction.
He is burning in Hell.

Piano Rolls

Tranströmer had a stroke.
His right arm was useless

and he struggled for words.
We tried to understand.

He stood up suddenly,
went over to the piano,

and played for his guests
music for the left hand.

*

The Mafia killed his father
for some reason—Cosa Nostra.

Then offered his mother
money. She walked away.

He was too young
to kill them, so he smiles.

I have seen him at work,
hammering and twisting metal.

*

Life will soon be over,
you think.

No sooner do you
think so, than

she comes bustling in
with a pretty knee

and a teapot, humming
"Amazing Grace."

*

Buster was my dog.
They sent me to boarding school.

When I came back he was gone.
They never told me why.

They must have got rid of him.
This is the worst thing

that ever happened to me.
It was worse than the war.

*

She died in her sleep,
an age of voyages

in interstellar space,
world changing policies,

a war fought over oil.
But nothing changes

the color of her eyes,
the corner of a smile.

The Sadness of Laforgue

Another book! Soulful stories,
Far from the madding crowd,
Far from salutes and money,
And little language games.

One more of my pierrots dead
From chronic instability,
A heart full of dandyism
Adrift in a foolish body.

The gods are fading fast.
Ah, every day it's worse.
I've done my share, and depend
On the bishop for support.

Petition

With the agony of crossings without water
But pomp and circumstance of a farewell,

Never outspoken, or fist on hip,
Love runs away,
Simple and faithless
As a smile and shake of the hand.

On armor plated orange flowers,
She faintly spreads
The Mystic Rose
When she sees our weddings
Of sexes delivered whole,
Running in a waltz
To the common
Ditch.

Sundays

My fate has no father, vespers killed the bells,
And those pianos never tired of playing . . .
Oh! to rise, to explain my apostleship to them!
Oh! at least turn the pages for them, be there!
Console them! (I have pocketfuls of consolations).

The pianos are closed, one alone, in grief, persists.
Oh! whoever you are, sister, in rags, kneeling
To kiss the edge of your dress, in abandon,
Provided you follow me, saying: "Pardon!"
Pardon, sir, but I love someone, I am her cousin!

Oh! but I am very unhappy on this earth!
And so unhappy for not being elsewhere!
Far from this instructed, raging century.
It is there that I have a little inner space
With one like myself one has to make . . .

A gaunt one who speaks,
Eyes hallucinating with virginal glories,
Soul making without harm
And a flask of English salt!

One who made me forget
My art and its absurd saturnalia,
Poking the fire, gauche vestal,
With a pillow over my ears . . .

And his sublime
Gaze
Like my rhyme

Does not permit the least doubt in the question.

Lottie Hasn't Been Feeling Well Lately

She slept all day long
and didn't eat a thing.

So I took a walk with her.
She got her appetite back.

I don't know what I would do
if anything happened to Lottie.

She is the most beautiful Beagle
in America. But beauty isn't all.

Character is more important
in the long run.

Three swans came by today,
all of them looking for a handout.

Lottie got to her feet and she *growled*.
The swans kept their distance.

Beagles and dogs don't
travel with freeloaders.

Aston and Rosalind

Buying a House

We were living in a house
my father was thinking of buying.
A door suddenly opened
and who should come in
but my mother, Rosalind.
She was holding a revolver.
"Now Rosalind," he said.
He walked across the room
and took the gun from her hand.
She fell to the floor,
foaming at the mouth.
I was seven years old.
I thought she was mad.

Cosmetics

She flew to New York.
There was an opening
for cosmetics in Venezuela.
Helena Rubinstein gave her
a contract, then tried to break it.
She got a good lawyer and beat them.

She married a . . . Renato
who was good-looking,
and bought a house in Viareggio.
Not a house, a palazzo.
They called it Villa Rosalinda.

Not bad for a girl who was born
in Lutsk!

On the boat that was bringing her
to America she gave her last
kopec for a bowl of soup
and saved her sister's life.

On the Jitney

Trilling gives me a look
of mild exasperation.

Then I wake up. It's Monday.
I am on the Jitney.
Thank God I didn't miss it.
If I did what would I find to eat?
Pickles would hardly do it.

I have an exciting life.
Actually I do, with all my narrow
escapes. Taking books back to
the library before they are overdue
and I'm fined thirty or even sixty cents.

Another thing would be driving.
But I don't want to
talk about that.

Most of the people driving
are insane, filled with rage.
How did that start? Not just the men
but women too.
God help you if you get in the way.

So I gave up driving.
How do I get around?
I have some friends,
and the Jitney.

There is one thing I don't
like to think too much about.
The people on the Jitney
are old, and getting older.

They are nearly all women.
The women talk and laugh,
they seem to be enjoying the ride.

There are one or two men.
They bury themselves in the news,
and say goodbye. That is all.

Acknowledgments

Five Points: "The Catalogue," "Consolations";

Fulcrum: "My Life the Movie";

The Gettysburg Review: "In and About the House";

The Hudson Review: "An New Year's Child," "An Impasse," "Avalon," "Vivien in *The Waste Land*," "Beatrice," "Ishi," "Joan Crawford Was Right," "Mr. and Mrs. Yeats," "The Discovery of Silence," "Sentimental Education," "The Caprichos," "Chamber Music";

The New Criterion: "Suddenly";

The Southern Review: "A Spot on the Kitchen Floor," "The Glass Eel Gatherer," "The Omen."

About the Author

Educated at Munro College (Jamaica, West Indies) and at Columbia, where he received his doctorate, Louis Simpson has taught at Columbia, the University of California at Berkeley, and at the State University of New York at Stony Brook. Simpson is the author of eighteen books of poetry, including *The Owner of the House: New Collected Poems 1940–2001* (BOA Editions, 2003), which was a finalist for the National Book Award in Poetry. He has received the Rome Fellowship of the American Academy of Arts and Letters, a *Hudson Review* fellowship, Guggenheim Foundation fellowships, and the Pulitzer Prize. Simpson lives in Stony Brook, New York.

BOA Editions, Ltd.
American Poets Continuum Series

Colophon

Struggling Times, poems by Louis Simpson,
is set in Adobe Garamond, a digital font designed in 1989
by Robert Slimbach (1956–) based on the French Renaissance
roman types of Claude Garamond (ca. 1480–1561) and the italics
of Robert Granjon (1513–1589).

The publication of this book is made possible, in part,
by the special support of the following individuals:

Anonymous
Judith Bishop ▨ Alan & Nancy Cameros
Bernadette Catalana ▨ Gwen & Gary Conners
Wyn Cooper & Shawna Parker
Barb & Charlie Coté, in memory of Charlie Coté, Jr. (1987–2005)
Dale Davis & Michael Starenko
Peter & Suzanne Durant
Suressa & Richard Forbes
Pete & Bev French ▨ Judy & Dane Gordon
Kip & Debby Hale
William B. Hauser ▨ Bob & Willy Hursh
Peter & Robin Hursh
Nora A. Jones
X. J. & Dorothy M. Kennedy
Archie & Pat Kutz ▨ Jack & Gail Langerak
Rosemary & Lewis Lloyd
Francie & Robert Marx ▨ Jim Robie & Edith Matthai
Elissa & Ernie Orlando ▨ Boo Poulin
John Roche, in memory of Salvatore J. Parlato
Paul & Andrea Rubery
Steven O. Russell & Phyllis Rifkin-Russell
Vicki & Richard Schwartz ▨ Joel & Friederike Seligman
George & Bonnie Wallace
Michael Waters & Mihaela Moscaliuc
Pat & Mike Wilder ▨ Glenn & Helen William